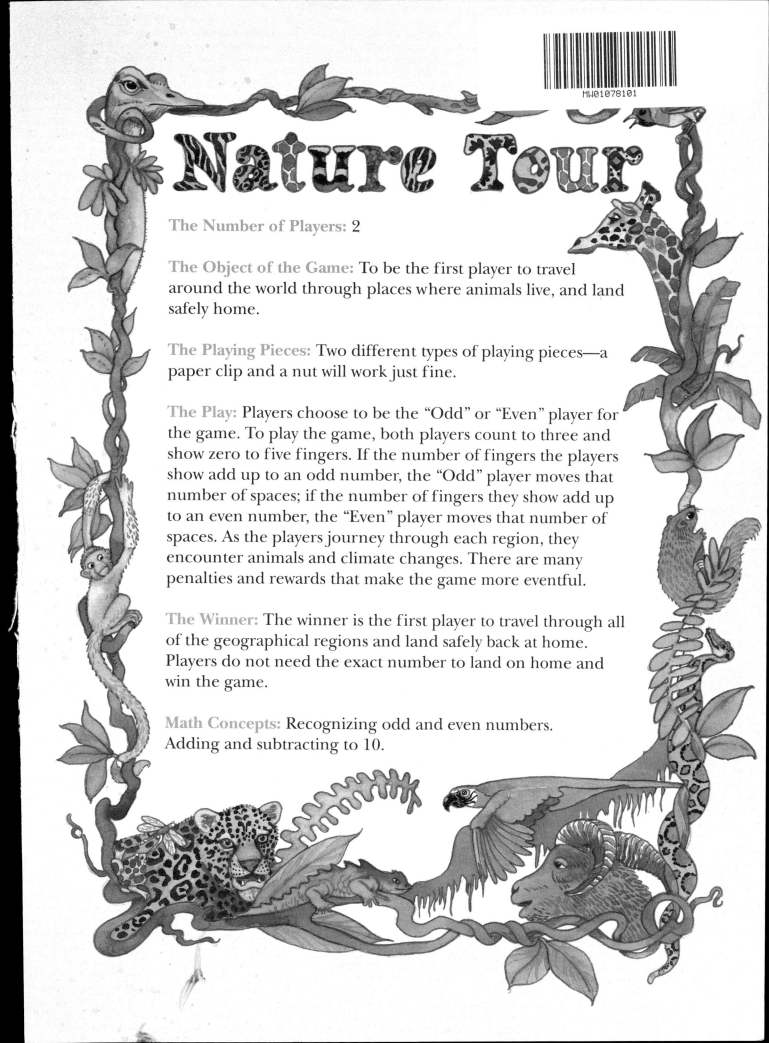

Nature Tour

The Number of Players: 2

The Object of the Game: To be the first player to travel around the world through places where animals live, and land safely home.

The Playing Pieces: Two different types of playing pieces—a paper clip and a nut will work just fine.

The Play: Players choose to be the "Odd" or "Even" player for the game. To play the game, both players count to three and show zero to five fingers. If the number of fingers the players show add up to an odd number, the "Odd" player moves that number of spaces; if the number of fingers they show add up to an even number, the "Even" player moves that number of spaces. As the players journey through each region, they encounter animals and climate changes. There are many penalties and rewards that make the game more eventful.

The Winner: The winner is the first player to travel through all of the geographical regions and land safely back at home. Players do not need the exact number to land on home and win the game.

Math Concepts: Recognizing odd and even numbers. Adding and subtracting to 10.

I LOVE MATH

RIGHT
IN YOUR
OWN
BACKYARD

NATURE MATH

TIME LIFE for Children ®

ALEXANDRIA, VIRGINIA

ALL ABOUT
I LOVE MATH

Learn a fun way to use a calculator. Skip to page 62.

Dear Parent,

The *I Love Math* series shows children that math is all around them in everything they do. It can be found at the grocery store, at a soccer game, in the kitchen, at the zoo, even in their own bodies. As you collect this series, each book will fill in another piece of your child's world, showing how math is a natural part of everyday activities.

What Is Math?

Math is much more than manipulating numbers; the goal of math education today is to help children become problem solvers. This means teaching kids to observe the world around them by looking for patterns and relationships, estimating, measuring, comparing, and using reasoning skills. From an early age, children do this naturally. They divide up cookies to share with friends, recognize shapes in pizza, measure how tall they have grown, or match colors and patterns as they dress themselves. Young children love math. But when math only takes the form of abstract formulas on worksheets, children begin to dislike it. The *I Love Math* series is designed to keep math natural and appealing.

How Do Children Learn Math?

Research has shown that children learn best by doing. Therefore, *I Love Math* is a hands-on, interactive learning experience. The math concepts are woven into stories in which entertaining characters invite your child to help them solve math challenges. Activities reinforce the concepts, and parent notes offer ways you and your child can have more fun with this program.

Be a honey and turn to page 6. We'll show you a quick way to estimate.

We have worked closely with math educators to include in these books a full range of math skills. As the series progresses, repetition of these skills in different formats will help your child master the basics of mathematical thinking.

What Will You Find in *Nature Math*?
In *Nature Math* you and your child will discover the rich array of math found right in your own backyard. Your child will count raindrops and learn to use a calendar; practice addition and simple multiplication with some three-leaf clover; search for nature's geometrical patterns, such as hexagons in a honeycomb and a tortoise shell; join two curious ants as they solve a mystery about temperature; and investigate the remarkable symmetry that appears throughout nature.

Once you and your child have read *Nature Math,* explore the great outdoors together—whether it's flowers in a city park, bugs in a mountain meadow, or even icy patterns on a frosty windowpane—and discover the incredible mathematical display that nature offers every day.

We hope you and your child will look at nature
in a new way and both will say:

I LOVE MATH!

The Editors
Time-Life for Children

Amazing, aren't we?
Turn to page 60 to see
how we measure up.

Table of Contents

FLOWER POWER

MATH FOCUS: NUMBERS AND ESTIMATION. By looking at pictures of countable and uncountable objects, children practice estimation, a time-saving skill underlying number awareness.

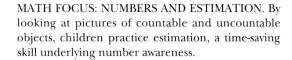

To help your child guess about how many flowers are in the big picture, have him or her count the flowers in the squared-off area. Your child can use this information to make a more accurate guess about the number of flowers in the entire picture.

MORE FUN. Your child can estimate how many books are on a bookcase in your home by first counting how many books there are in a small section or on one shelf and then making a guess based on that number.

Hide and Seek

MATH FOCUS: LOGICAL THINKING. Children consider more than one attribute of an object or animal in order to sort and to solve problems logically.

Tell your child to think about all three characteristics of each object or animal before deciding on the answer.

If you look closely, you should be able to . . .

find something that has a shell, moves slowly, and is brown.

find something that has a fuzzy tail, is brown, and purrs.

find something that flies, has a red head, and pecks at trees.

find something that has a shell, moves slowly, and is green.

find something that flies, is striped, and stings.

find something that is green, loves the water, and jumps.

find something that flies, has a red breast, and lays blue eggs.

MORE FUN. Help your child make up descriptions of other animals or objects in the picture and challenge family members to identify them.

ANSWERS. Snail; cat; woodpecker; turtle; bumblebee; frog; robin.

PATTERNS *in* NATURE

A pattern is a design that repeats over and over. Patterns in nature are fun to find. What pattern do you see in these snail shells?

This is a spiral pattern. It starts in the center and it goes on and on. . . . .

MATH FOCUS: GEOMETRY AND PATTERNS. By recognizing, duplicating, and describing patterns in nature, your child becomes familiar with some of the shapes and patterns that form the basis for geometry. The ability to identify and predict patterns is central to higher-level mathematical learning such as analyzing data and solving for a missing number in an algebraic equation.

Let's go hunting for spirals. When you find one, start in the center and trace the spiral with your finger.

Clockwise: FIDDLEHEAD FERN, BIGHORN RAM, NAUTILUS SHELL, SATELLITE VIEW OF HURRICANE

MORE FUN. Play "Guess My Pattern" with your child. Describe one of the patterns shown here and ask your child to guess the name of it. Then ask your child to describe a different pattern for you to name. Take turns until all the patterns have been named.

This is a branching pattern.

This is a branching pattern.

is a branching pattern.

is a branching pattern.

pattern.

Trace these branching patterns. Put your finger at the beginning of the long center line. Go all the way to the end. Then go back and trace the shorter branching lines.

Clockwise: DRAGONFLY, LEAF, CARIBOU, TREE, LIGHTNING

13

This pattern is different from a spiral.
Can you see why?

Here is a spiral.

Here is this pattern.

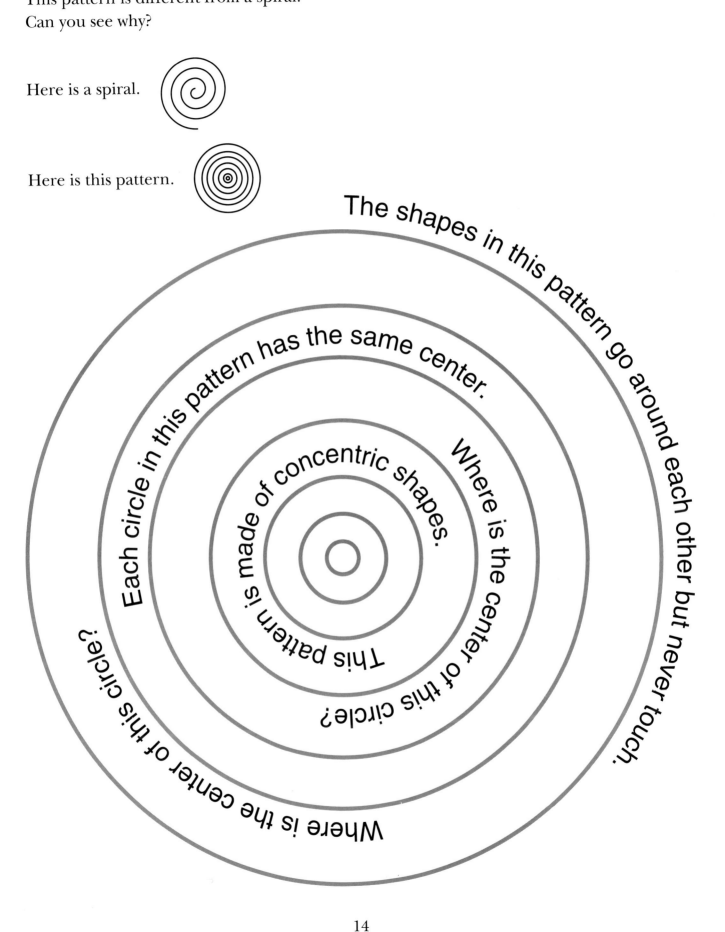

The shapes in this pattern go around each other but never touch.

Each circle in this pattern has the same center.

This pattern is made of concentric shapes.

Where is the center of this circle?

Where is the center of this circle?

14

What pattern can you see in
each of these pictures? Trace
the pattern with your finger.

Clockwise: GREEN RAZORFISH, WATER DROPLET AND
RIPPLES, PINE-TREE RINGS, BUCKEYE BUTTERFLY

You know the name of this design, don't you?

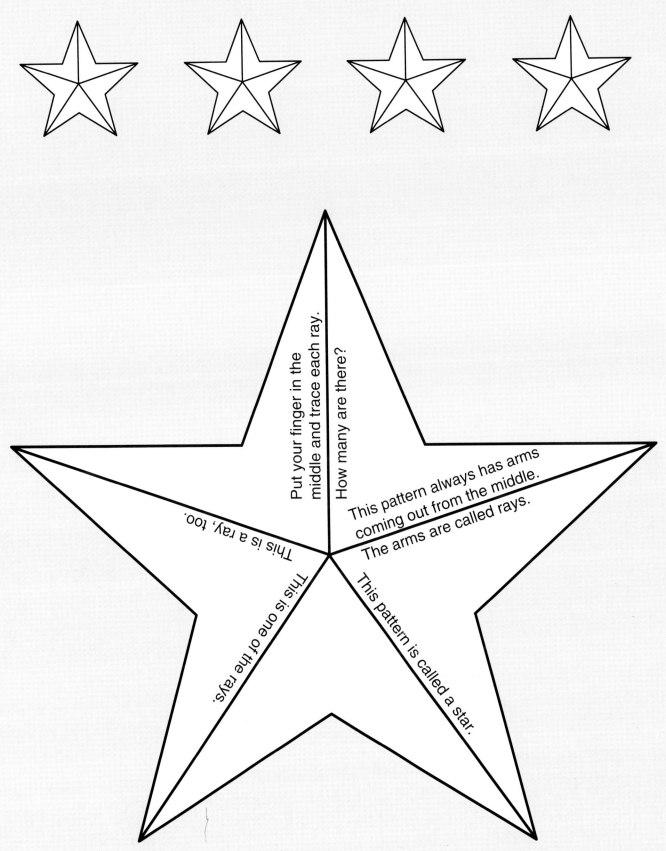

Put your finger in the middle and trace each ray.

How many are there?

This pattern always has arms coming out from the middle. The arms are called rays.

This is a ray, too.

This is one of the rays.

This pattern is called a star.

What pattern do you see in
each of these pictures?
Which pictures show an animal?
Which pictures show a plant?

Clockwise: SAND DOLLAR, STAR FRUIT, SEA STAR,
MARSH PINK FLOWER

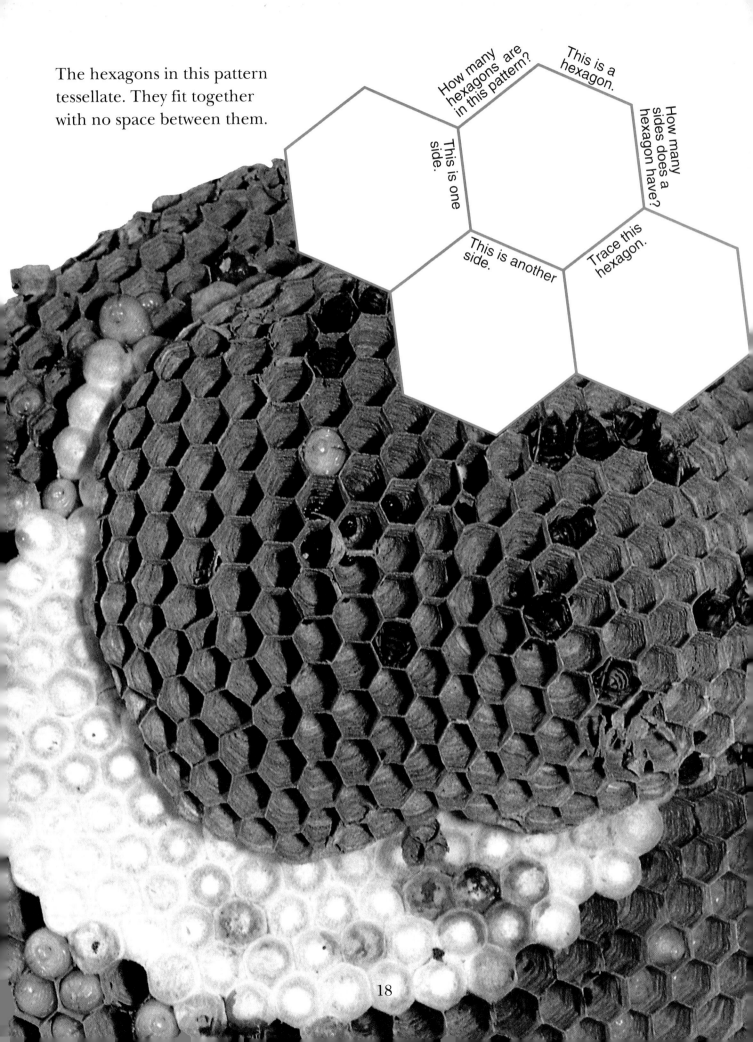

The hexagons in this pattern tessellate. They fit together with no space between them.

How many hexagons are in this pattern?

This is a hexagon.

This is one side.

How many sides does a hexagon have?

This is another side.

Trace this hexagon.

18

Which picture shows a busy
beehive? Which one shows a
beautiful crystal? Can you find
a tsetse fly and a magnified
picture of its eye?

What do the beehive, the crystal,
and the fly's eye have in
common?

Patterns, Patterns, Everywhere
Patterns, Patterns, Everywhere
Patterns, Patterns, Everywhere

How many pictures show a branching pattern?

Which pictures show a spiral pattern?

Can you find a hexagon pattern?

Do you see something with a star pattern?

Look for concentric circles here and also in your mirror.

MATH FOCUS: PATTERNS. In searching for patterns in nature, your child will begin to develop an understanding of and appreciation for the mathematical structure in nature.
For centuries, scholars have pondered nature's mathematical perfection. But none yet has unlocked the secret of why a spiral galaxy, a ram's horns, and a crashing wave share the same shape, or why a honeybee chooses the same six-sided structure as an emerald crystal for its honeycomb.

Choose two of the pictures.
How are they alike?
How are they different?

MORE FUN. You and your child can take a walk around your neighborhood and look for patterns in nature. Try to discover some not shown here.

21

MAKE YOUR OWN PATTERNS

Make a spiral.
Start in the center of a piece of paper.

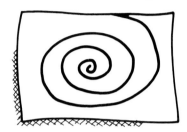

Draw a line around and around, to the edge of the paper. Start at the edge and cut on the line. Cut off the bottom. Lift the center and hang up your spiral.

Make a branching pattern.
Use a leaf with branching veins.

Place it vein side up.

Cover the leaf with a piece of paper. Color the paper over the leaf to see the branching pattern.

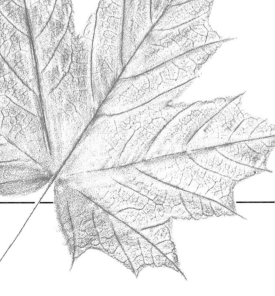

MATH FOCUS: PATTERNS. By creating their own patterns, children get hands-on experience of the regularities found in shapes and designs.

Make a concentric circle pattern.
Get a large plate, a small plate, and a glass.

Trace around the large plate on a piece of paper. Then put the small plate inside the circle you made. Trace around it.

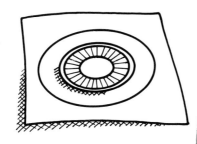

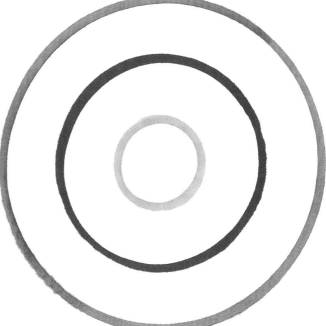

Do the same with the glass. Try to make all the circles have the same center.

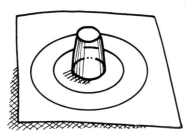

Make a star pattern.
Ask an adult to cut an apple across its middle.

Draw a picture of the star you see in the center. Then make a star print. Put some paint or ketchup on a plate. Put the cut side of the apple in the paint or ketchup.

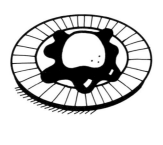

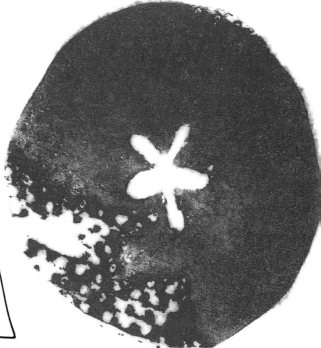

Press the cut side of the apple on a paper towel. Lift the apple. There's your star pattern again.

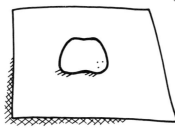

Have available drawing paper, crayons, scissors, a paper plate, tempera paint or ketchup, a paper towel, an apple, and a small knife. After your child has cut out the spiral, tell him or her that it is now called a spiral helix.

MORE FUN. Have your child challenge family members to guess the name of each pattern he or she has made.

MATH FOCUS: PLANE SHAPES. By watching a spider connect dots, children learn to recognize and identify a geometric shape by the number of corners and sides it has.

After your child counts the number of sides for each shape, have him or her tell you how many corners each shape has.

MORE FUN. Go outside with your child and look for spider webs. Name the different shapes you see. See if the shape of the web is determined by where the spider chooses to build its web.

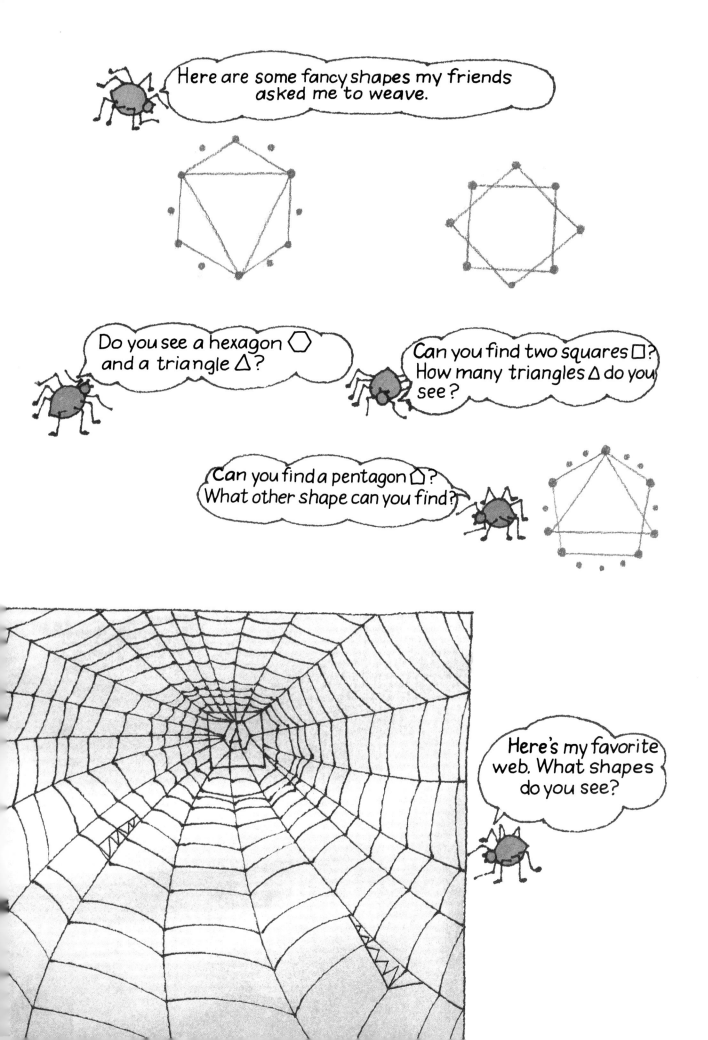

Place a piece of tracing paper over these circles of dots. Then follow my friends' directions.

Connect every other dot in each circle of dots. What shapes do you find?

In the circle of 12 dots, connect every third dot. What shape do you find?

Make up your own directions. What shapes and designs do you find? This hint might help you: Always skip the same number of dots.

HAVE FUN!

27

The TRASH CAN CAPER

Professor Guesser was out for a ride one beautiful Monday morning when she spotted her old friend Tracker the bloodhound.

"Professor Guesser!" called Tracker. "You're just who I deed! I'b happy to see you."

"You sound awful!" said Professor Guesser. "What's the matter?"

"I have a cold id by doze. I can't sbell a thing. Ah, ahh, AHH-CHOO! I can't hear, and I can't bark." Tracker let out a pitiful, "Woof, ah, ah, ruff, ah, ahh, AAHH-CHOO!"

Professor Guesser gave the unhappy hound a handkerchief and a pat on the back. "That is a bad cold. You should be resting."

"I can't rest when there's a cribe to solve," sniffed Tracker. "Just look at by backyard. Subwud kceps docking over the trash cans. But I can't sbell who it is, or bark to scare theb away."

"What a mess!" said Professor Guesser. "You really are in trouble."

MATH FOCUS: STATISTICS, THE CALENDAR, PATTERNS, AND LOGICAL THINKING. By listening to this mystery story, children learn how to solve problems by using data, the days of the week, patterns, and thinking skills.

You and your child (or another family member) can take the parts of the characters and read the story out loud. Point out the tops of the file cards on page 32. Have your child name the animals that are scavengers and the ones that are active at night.

"Please help be solve the bistery," begged Tracker. "I have a reputation to protect."

Professor Guesser pulled out a notebook. "OK. Let's get the facts," she said. "When did the crimes occur?"

"After dark, about dide o'clock or so," answered Tracker.

"Nine o'clock at night. Hmm, the culprit, or criminal, never strikes during the day. Were the trash cans hit every night?" asked Professor Guesser.

"They were docked over six tibes so far this bonth: Bunday the first, Wednesday the third, Friday the fifth, Bunday the eighth, Wednesday the tenth, and Friday the twelfth," replied Tracker.

"Let me circle the days on this calendar to see when the crimes were committed," said Professor Guesser. "If the criminal repeated the crime on the same days each week, we can find a pattern and then use the pattern to figure out when the culprit will strike again."

Sunday	Monday	Tuesday	Wednesday	Thursday	Friday	Saturday
	(1)	2	(3)	4	(5)	6
7	(8)	9	(10)	11	(12)	13
14	15	16	17	18	19	20
21	22	23	24	25	26	27
28	29	30				

What pattern do you see on the calendar?
When do you predict the culprit will strike next?

MORE FUN. Help your child write a file card for your family pet or for another animal.

"It looks like our culprit might strike again tonight," deduced Professor Guesser, looking at her calendar.

"But why would subwud want to turn over trash cans?" asked Tracker.

"Good question," said Professor Guesser. "We need to figure out the motive. Someone probably turned over the cans because they wanted what was inside."

"But that's garbage!" said Tracker.

"Exactly," said Professor Guesser. "There are some animals, called scavengers, who eat food that others leave behind—or garbage."

"Great!" cheered Tracker. "We've got this case solved!"

"I don't know if we have enough information yet," said Professor Guesser. "But let's write down everything we know so far."

The Trash Can Caper:

Who is the culprit?....A scavenger

What is the crime?.... Knocking over trash cans

When does the crime occur? ..... After 9 o'clock P.M.

Where does the crime occur? .... Backyards around the neighborhood

How is the crime committed? ..... By giving the cans a big push

Why does the culprit commit the crime? ..... It's probably hungry

Is there enough information on this chart to solve the mystery?

What other information might the professor need to solve the mystery?

30

"As I suspected," sighed Professor Guesser, "we need more information to solve this mystery. But I do have an idea. Let's stake out your backyard tonight."

"This is no tibe for a picnic," said Tracker.

"We're not going to eat a steak in the backyard. We're going to stake out, or hide in, the backyard tonight to see who is turning over the trash," explained the professor.

"I dew that," huffed Tracker.

"We should know what to expect so we can be properly prepared," said Professor Guesser. "What kind of animals live around this neighborhood?"

"There are sub skunks, a squirrel or two, opossums, bats, vultures, a raccoon, three deer, and a fabily of foxes," replied Tracker.

Professor Guesser wrote the list of suspects in her notebook. "I'll meet you back here tonight at 8 o'clock. I have some research to do before the stakeout."

Professor Guesser put on her helmet and rode back to her office.

"Let's see if I can find some information to help me narrow the list of suspects," said Professor Guesser, looking through her files. "I need to know which of the animals on my list are scavengers and are also active at night."

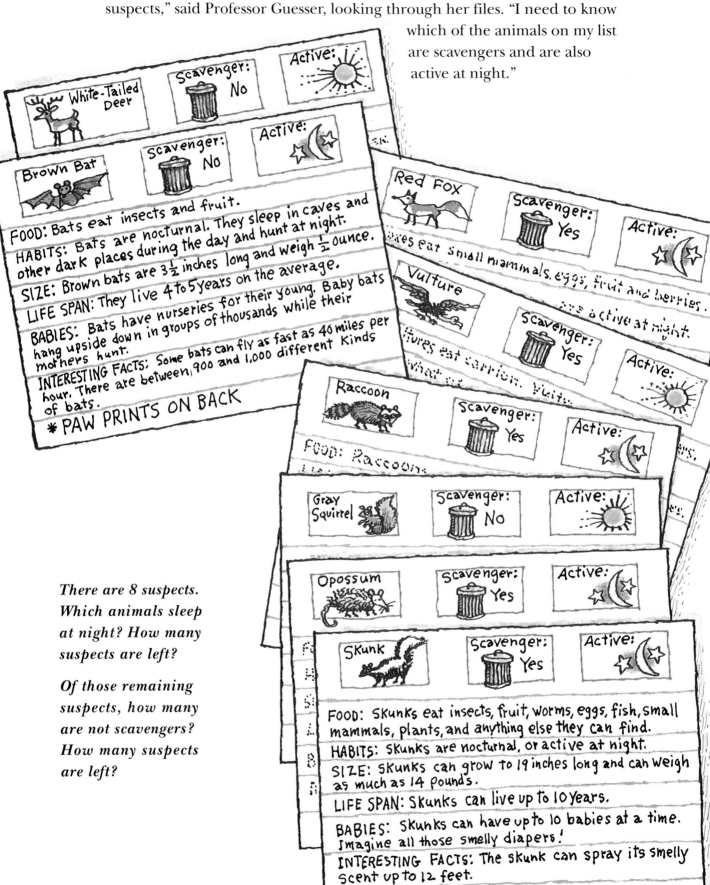

White-Tailed Deer — Scavenger: No — Active: ☀

Brown Bat — Scavenger: No — Active: ☾

FOOD: Bats eat insects and fruit.
HABITS: Bats are nocturnal. They sleep in caves and other dark places during the day and hunt at night.
SIZE: Brown bats are 3½ inches long and weigh ½ ounce.
LIFE SPAN: They live 4 to 5 years on the average.
BABIES: Bats have nurseries for their young. Baby bats hang upside down in groups of thousands while their mothers hunt.
INTERESTING FACTS: Some bats can fly as fast as 40 miles per hour. There are between 900 and 1,000 different kinds of bats.
* PAW PRINTS ON BACK

Red Fox — Scavenger: Yes — Active: ☾
...es eat small mammals, eggs, fruit and berries.

Vulture — Scavenger: Yes — Active: ☀
...are active at night.
...tures eat carrion. Vultu...

Raccoon — Scavenger: Yes — Active: ☾
FOOD: Raccoon...

Gray Squirrel — Scavenger: No — Active: ☀

Opossum — Scavenger: Yes — Active: ☾

Skunk — Scavenger: Yes — Active: ☾
FOOD: Skunks eat insects, fruit, worms, eggs, fish, small mammals, plants, and anything else they can find.
HABITS: Skunks are nocturnal, or active at night.
SIZE: Skunks can grow to 19 inches long and can weigh as much as 14 pounds.
LIFE SPAN: Skunks can live up to 10 years.
BABIES: Skunks can have up to 10 babies at a time. Imagine all those smelly diapers!
INTERESTING FACTS: The skunk can spray its smelly scent up to 12 feet.
* PAW PRINTS ON BACK

There are 8 suspects. Which animals sleep at night? How many suspects are left?

Of those remaining suspects, how many are not scavengers? How many suspects are left?

Professor Guesser met Tracker at 8 o'clock that evening, just as the sun was about to set. The creatures of the day were settling down for a good night's sleep, and the animals of the night were beginning to stir.

"I looked up some information about all the animals that live in your neighborhood. I've narrowed the list of suspects to four," said Professor Guesser.

"Is each one a scavenger?" asked Tracker.

"Each one scavenges from time to time," answered the professor.

"And is each awake at dight?" asked Tracker.

"Yes, each suspect is a nocturnal animal—that means each one is awake at night," said Professor Guesser. "The trash can culprit is either . . ."

Which four animals could be the culprit?

". . . a skunk, an opossum, a raccoon, or a fox!"

She handed Tracker a big net. "Get ready. When the culprit strikes, we'll jump out and catch it in our nets." They crouched in the bushes and waited anxiously.

It grew darker and darker. Soon they couldn't even see the trash can.

At 9 o'clock sharp, Professor Guesser heard footsteps and the rustling of leaves. Someone sniffed the trash can. Then there was a loud thump and the terrible smell of trash spilling on the ground.

"That's the culprit," whispered the professor. "On the count of 3, we'll nab it. 1, 2, 3, GO!"

Professor Guesser sprang out, and Tracker pounced right behind her. There was a great struggle as they thrashed in the trash, banging and rattling the can.

"I've got 'em," wheezed Tracker.

"You've got me, Tracker!" shouted Professor Guesser.

In the bushes the culprit cried, "Better luck next time!"

"Oh, no! The culprit got away!" said Professor Guesser unhappily.

In the morning, Professor Guesser and Tracker went to the backyard to clean up the mess they had made the night before. As Tracker unhappily gathered trash, the professor searched the yard for a clue.

"Tracker!" she shouted suddenly, "I've found something!"

"I don't see abything!" sniffed Tracker. "Just sub bessy paw prints all over the yard."

"That's right," said Professor Guesser. "These prints were left by our criminal! Perhaps we can match them to the prints in my Nature Files." She pulled the files from her purse. "And this trail of paw prints should lead us to the culprit."

"Let's go!" said Tracker.

Who do you think the culprit is?

35

Professor Guesser and Tracker followed the tracks. At the end of the trail was a very fat and sleepy raccoon.

"You should be ashamed for turning over the neighborhood trash cans," said Professor Guesser.

"But that's not a crime. Raccoons who live in neighborhoods always turn over the trash," said the raccoon, rubbing her drowsy eyes. "If I lived in the woods, I would have plenty of other food to eat, and I wouldn't have to scavenge from trash cans."

"That's it!" said the professor. "I'll give you a ride to the woods. There will be plenty of food, and you won't have to bother Tracker anymore!"

"It's a deal!" said the raccoon, hopping on the back of the motorcycle.

"Thank you, Professor Guesser!" shouted Tracker as they roared off. "Ah, ah, AHH-CHOO!"

"Think nothing of it, Tracker. Now, we're off to the woods!" Professor Guesser called out to the raccoon. "You were born to be wild!"

FILE FACTS

FOOD: Skunks eat insects, fruit, worms, eggs, fish, small mammals, plants, and anything else they can find.

HABITS: Skunks are nocturnal, or active at night.

SIZE: Skunks can grow to 19 inches long and can weigh as much as 14 pounds.

LIFE SPAN: Skunks can live up to 10 years.

BABIES: Skunks can have up to 10 babies at a time. Imagine all those smelly diapers!

INTERESTING FACTS: The skunk can spray its smelly scent up to 12 feet.

✳ PAW PRINTS ON BACK

Skunk PAW PRINTS

Which animal can weigh more than the other? How much more?

Which animal can live as much as 4 years longer than the other?

Which animal's babies are called cubs?

How much longer can a raccoon grow than a skunk?

Which animal can have up to 10 babies at a time?

When could you see a skunk, during the day or at night?

Is a raccoon a vegetarian?

How many toes are on one skunk foot?

Raccoon PAW PRINTS

FOOD: Raccoons eat frogs, insects, mice, crayfish, worms, fruit, nuts, vegetables, and human garbage.

HABITS: Raccoons are nocturnal, or active at night.

SIZE: Raccoons can weigh up to 26 pounds and can grow to 26 inches long.

LIFE SPAN: Raccoons live about 6 years.

BABIES: Baby raccoons are called cubs.

INTERESTING FACTS: The scientific name for the raccoon means "the washer." But raccoons don't actually wash their food. In the wild, raccoons get much of their food from the water. In captivity, they drop their food in their water dishes, simulating food-finding conditions from the wild.

✳ PAW PRINTS ON BACK

Can you detect the correct insect?

Meet the Beetles

Where is the blue snout beetle? The rest of it is blue, too.

Try to find the eyed elater beetle. It looks like it has two big black eyes with a white ring around each. But they are just markings.

Decide which insect is the diving beetle. Its two back legs are bigger than its four front legs. It is black with a brown edge. Its antennae are delicate looking.

Can you find the Japanese beetle without a clue?

Find the Colorado potato beetle. It is small and has a lot of yellow and black stripes on its wing covers.

Find the violin beetle. It has very long antennae and it's big and brown. How do you think it got its name?

Where is the dung beetle? It is shiny green and has a big spot near its head. Its colors are like a Japanese beetle's but it is bigger.

MATH FOCUS: LOGICAL THINKING. Children use logical reasoning to match each beetle's description with its picture.

Tell your child that each beetle must have all of the characteristics (attributes) given, and that he or she can eliminate beetles that have only one or two.

38

Figure out which one is the Hercules beetle. It's shiny and looks as if its wing covers were splattered with ink. It has a long snout and is the second-biggest beetle on these pages.

The biggest black-and-yellow beetle on this page is the American carrion beetle. It has short antennae. The one with lots of black and yellow stripes and long antennae is the locust borer longhorn. The net-winged beetle is the other black-and-yellow beetle. How do you think it got its name?

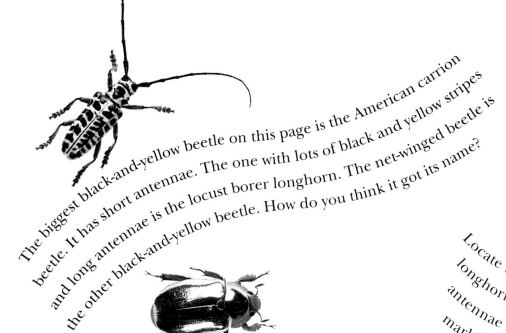

Locate the cottonwood borer longhorn. It has long, bumpy antennae and black-and-white markings.

One of the green beetles is the green dung beetle. It has short antennae and black legs. The one with green legs is called the golden-striped beetle. Can you see why?

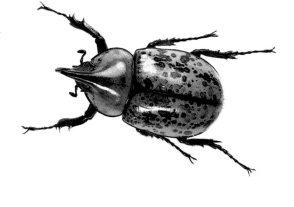

Where is the shining golden leaf beetle?

MORE FUN. Your child can catch a ladybug or a Japanese beetle and compare it to the beetles shown on this page. Note that the beetles pictured here are life-size.

MIRROR MIRROR

MIRROR MIRROR

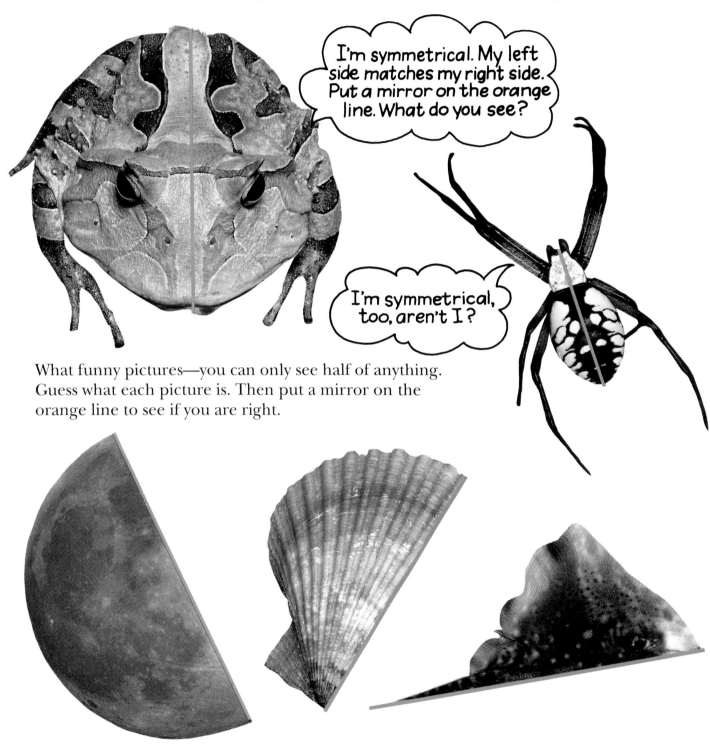

I'm symmetrical. My left side matches my right side. Put a mirror on the orange line. What do you see?

I'm symmetrical, too, aren't I?

What funny pictures—you can only see half of anything. Guess what each picture is. Then put a mirror on the orange line to see if you are right.

MATH FOCUS: SYMMETRY. Children learn to understand and recognize symmetry by using a mirror to create the illusion of a whole object from half a picture.

40

Help your child place the edge of a small pocket mirror on the orange line of symmetry of each picture so that the reflection in the mirror creates the image of the complete object, person, or animal.

Am I symmetrical? Is my right side just like my left side?

MORE FUN. Ask your child to look through this book and in nature for other objects and animals that look symmetrical.

41

RIGHT IN YOUR OWN
BACK YARD

The early spring wind whipped through the grass. It almost blew away the two worker ants who were out searching for food for their ant colony.

"I've never seen such a windstorm!" said Star to her co-worker, Jetta. "Hold on tight!" They bent their heads and clung to a bush.

So neither Star nor Jetta saw the strange thing fall to the grass.

MATH FOCUS: TEMPERATURE. By watching a thermometer during different seasons of the year, children learn how temperature is measured.

After a while the wind calmed down and the ants crawled down off the bush. Jetta saw the thing first.

"Look, Star," she said. "What's this?"

But Star could only look and wonder. Both ants crawled very carefully around the thing. Now and then one of them touched it gingerly with one of her six legs. Then Star, followed by the cautious Jetta, crawled right up onto the shiny glass with the red line in it.

"I have an idea," Star said. "Come on, let's go home!"

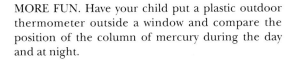
MORE FUN. Have your child put a plastic outdoor thermometer outside a window and compare the position of the column of mercury during the day and at night.

Star and Jetta told all the ants in the colony about the thing they'd discovered. Nobody could figure out what it was or what it did. Star explained her idea and all the curious worker ants volunteered to help her put her idea into action.

All morning long the ants worked. Pulling and tugging, they dragged the thing past the newly planted garden. The midday sun was shining high overhead by the time they had carried the thing to their ant hill next to the peony plants.

"Now what?" asked Jetta. "You can't possibly expect to fit this into our nest."

"Of course not," said Star. "We can prop it up on that rock where we can watch it. Maybe then we can figure out what it is."

By the end of the day, the ants had pushed and pulled the mysterious object until it leaned securely against a rock right next to the front door of their nest.

"Look at the red line," said Star. "It looks different from the way it looked at noon."

Most of the ants paid no attention to her. They were going inside the ant hill to get out of the cool breeze. But Jetta was fascinated.

"You're right," she said. "The red line is shorter. It reached the 80 mark at noon and now it only reaches 50. I wonder why."

The two ants sat up all night—watching and wondering.

How many marks shorter was the red line at the end of the day than at noon?

For days the ants went in and out of the ant hill past the thing on their way to get food or water. Star and Jetta and some of the other curious worker ants watched the thing. But only Star and Jetta really talked about it. They even crawled out at night, when the moonlight was bright enough, to see how far up or down the red line had moved. But they couldn't figure out why it happened.

One day, while the children splashed in their pool, Jetta crawled over to check the red line. She tilted her head way up to see the top.

"Those black marks on the side of the red line must be important," said Jetta.

"What are those black marks?" wondered Star.

A nearby inchworm said, "The black marks remind me of the ones on a ruler. Rulers measure things. These black marks must be for measuring, too."

"Thanks for your help!" called Star.

"But what can that red line be for?" sighed Jetta.

"Hey, I know an expert on red!" Star exclaimed. "Ruby the hummingbird. Next time I see her, I'll ask."

PUMPKINS

100
90
80
70
60
50
40
32
30
20
10
0

47

What can a ruler measure? What do you think the red line is for?

It was early fall before Star and Jetta saw Ruby.

"Hi, Ruby," said Star. "We're really puzzled by something that is red. Maybe you can help us. Fly over and take a look."

Ruby hovered above the thing. "Well, when I see a lot of red, that usually means 'summer' to me," she said. "There are more red things around in the summer: cherries, strawberries, and all kinds of flowers. The color red helps me tell the difference between summer and winter. The other way, of course, is by how hot or cold it is. It's kind of cold right now—time for me to get back to my nest for the night! Good-bye."

"You know, Ruby may have given us a clue," Jetta said. "The red line was much longer during the summer. It sometimes reached 90."

"And now it hardly ever goes above 40," Star agreed.

Why do you think the red line was longer in the summer than it is in this picture?

Several weeks later, the ants saw an amazing thing.

"Look at the white stuff!" Star exclaimed.

"And look at the thing!" Jetta added. "The red line is under the big black mark at 32—it's never been that low before."

The ants crawled out to investigate the white stuff and the thing. Suddenly a huge shadow fell across the ground. A booming voice said, "There's our outdoor thermometer! I wondered what happened to it. I'll hang it back up next to the kitchen window. Then we can look at it each morning and know how cold it is outside." A giant hand picked up the thing, and the shadow moved away.

"Well, now we know what the thing is," Jetta said.

Star answered, "And I know it's too cold to stay out here talking. We belong inside."

"Let's go!" said Jetta.

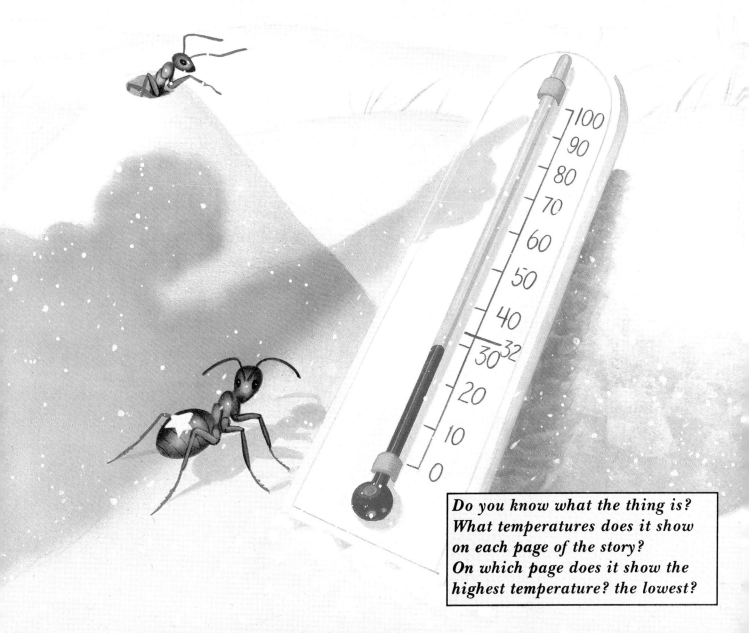

Do you know what the thing is?
What temperatures does it show on each page of the story?
On which page does it show the highest temperature? the lowest?

MATH FOCUS: TEMPERATURE. By using a thermometer to compare the temperatures of hot and cold water, children have a hands-on measuring experience and learn to associate degree readings with specific temperatures.

MORE FUN. Have your child put the bowl of water outside for a few hours and guess whether the temperature will go up or down. Then see if he or she is correct.

CLOVER TIME

Here is a clover and a tiny flea.
Tell how many leaves you see.

Here are 2 clovers and a bumblebee.
Please count the leaves carefully.

Here are 3 clovers in sunny weather.
How many leaves are there altogether?

MATH FOCUS: ADDITION AND MULTIPLICATION.
By counting groups of objects with the same amount in each group, children begin to employ time-saving strategies, such as skipping saying the number of objects already counted or "skip counting," that are linked to multiplication readiness. Your child can use buttons or other counters to make groups of 3 to represent each 3-leaf clover. For the last picture, help your child make groups of 4 to represent each 4-leaf clover.

Here are 4 clovers straight and tall.
How many leaves are there in all?

5 green clovers in the breeze.
How many leaves, if you please?

Uh-oh! This rhyme is over.
Here is a bunch of 4-leaf clovers!

MORE FUN. Ask your child to guess how many
leaves are in the border. Then count them together.

53

THE YELLOW SLICKER

Hi! I'm a yellow slicker, and I love to go out in the rain.

Here's a calendar that shows all of the months of the year, and all of the days of each month. Each raindrop represents a rainy day. Can you tell which days it rained?

Here are some questions I want to ask. Maybe you can think of others.

JANUARY

SUN	MON	TUES	WED	THUR	FRI	SAT
						1
2	3	4	5	6	7	8
9	10	11	12	13	14	15
16	17	18	19	20	21	22
23	24	25	26	27	28	29
30	31					

FEBRUARY

SUN	MON	TUES	WED	THUR	FRI	SAT
		1	2	3	4	5
6	7	8	9	10	11	12
13	14	15	16	17	18	19
20	21	22	23	24	25	26
27	28					

MARCH

SUN	MON	TUES	WED	THUR	FRI	SAT
		1	2	3	4	5
6	7	8	9	10	11	12
13	14	15	16	17	18	19
20	21	22	23	24	25	26
27	28	29	30	31		

JULY

SUN	MON	TUES	WED	THUR	FRI	SAT
					1	2
3	4	5	6	7	8	9
10	11	12	13	14	15	16
17	18	19	20	21	22	23
24	25	26	27	28	29	30
31						

AUGUST

SUN	MON	TUES	WED	THUR	FRI	SAT
	1	2	3	4	5	6
7	8	9	10	11	12	13
14	15	16	17	18	19	20
21	22	23	24	25	26	27
28	29	30	31			

SEPTEMBER

SUN	MON	TUES	WED	THUR	FRI	SAT
				1	2	3
4	5	6	7	8	9	10
11	12	13	14	15	16	17
18	19	20	21	22	23	24
25	26	27	28	29	30	

Did it rain more days in June or in September?

Would it have been better to have a vacation at the beach in June, July, or August?

Would July 5 have been a good day to go to the beach?

MATH FOCUS: THE CALENDAR, STATISTICS, ADDITION, AND SUBTRACTION. Children become familiar with a calendar and learn to read a related graph by solving problems about the days and months of the year.

54

Discuss with your child how this calendar is organized. Help him or her to read the names of the months in order and then to say the names of the days of the week in order.

On rainy days, people say "It's good weather for ducks."

Which month had the best "duck weather"?

Which month had the fewest rainy days?

How many Saturdays did it rain in March?

How many Saturdays did it rain in the whole year?

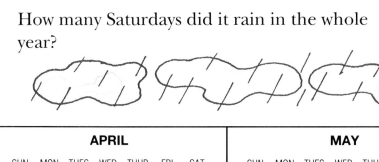

APRIL

SUN	MON	TUES	WED	THUR	FRI	SAT
					1	2 🌢
3	4	5 🌢	6	7	8 🌢	9
10	11	12	13 🌢	14	15	16
17	18 🌢	19 🌢	20	21	22 🌢	23
24	25	26	27 🌢	28	29	30

MAY

SUN	MON	TUES	WED	THUR	FRI	SAT
1 🌢	2	3	4	5 🌢	6	7
8	9	10	11	12	13	14
15	16 🌢	17	18	19 🌢	20	21
22	23	24	25 🌢	26	27	28
29 🌢	30 🌢	31				

JUNE

SUN	MON	TUES	WED	THUR	FRI	SAT
			1 🌢	2	3	4 🌢
5	6	7 🌢	8	9	10	11
12 🌢	13	14	15	16	17	18
19	20	21	22	23	24	25
26	27	28	29	30		

OCTOBER

SUN	MON	TUES	WED	THUR	FRI	SAT
						1
2	3	4 🌢	5	6 🌢	7	8
9	10	11	12		14	15
16 🌢	17	18	19 🌢	20 🌢	21 🌢	22
23	24	25	26	27	28	29
30	31 🌢					

NOVEMBER

SUN	MON	TUES	WED	THUR	FRI	SAT
		1	2	3	4	5
6	7	8 🌢	9	10 🌢	11	12
13	14 🌢	15	16	17	18	19
20	21	22	23 🌢	24	25	26
27 🌢	28	29 🌢	30			

DECEMBER

SUN	MON	TUES	WED	THUR	FRI	SAT
				1	2	3 🌢
4	5	6	7 🌢	8	9 🌢	10
11 🌢	12	13	14	15	16	17
18	19 🌢	20	21	22	23	24
25	26	27	28	29	30	31

Did it rain on Halloween?

Did it rain on your birthday?

How many days did it rain in December?

How many days did it not rain in December?

MORE FUN. Find a calendar your child can use to keep track of rainy days in your area.

NUMBER OF RAINY DAYS

10
9
8
7
6
5
4
3
2
1

MONTHS

| January | February | March | April | May |

Here's a graph with a raindrop for every rainy day that's marked on the calendar. I've stacked up each month's rainy days so we can compare them. The graph makes it easy to see which months had more rain than others.

June	July	August	September	October	November	December

How many more days did it rain in November than
in December?
How many days did it rain in February and March?
How many days did it rain in the whole year?

MIX and MATCH FLOWER PATCH

Can you find two flowers with a total of nine petals? Can you find two other flowers with a total of nine petals?

Can you find two flowers with a total of ten petals? Can you find two other flowers with a total of ten petals?

Choose three flowers. How many petals do they have in all?

MATH FOCUS: ADDITION. Children practice addition by creating different combinations of flower petals to solve problems.

58

Help your child select flowers and count petals to answer each question. Suggest that your child solve each question several ways, using different flowers each time.

MORE FUN. Your child can create his or her own flower questions and challenge family members to solve them.

ANIMATH

Are there fish bigger than you?

An ocean sunfish is about 10 feet long.

Could an ocean sunfish take a bath in your tub?

Do you think there are fish longer than your house?

Maybe. The whale shark is about 60 feet long!

How many ocean sunfishes would you have to line up end to end to be as long as 1 whale shark?

What is one of the smallest animals you can think of?

The pygmy shrew is only about 3 inches long.

How many pygmy shrews could you line up end to end on a 12-inch ruler?

Could a pygmy shrew sit on your finger?

MATH FOCUS: ESTIMATION AND MEASUREMENT—
LENGTH, WEIGHT, AND HEIGHT. Children use fascinating number facts about animals to solve word problems.

Ask your child to guess the answer to each question and then help him or her find the actual answer, using a ruler when needed.

Could a giraffe walk through your door—without bumping its head?

The giraffe is the tallest animal. It can grow to be 18 feet tall!

Could a giraffe stand in your living room?

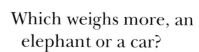

Which weighs more, an elephant or a car?

This African elephant weighs about 6 tons. The car only weighs about 1 ton.

How many cars weigh about as much as 1 African elephant?

Can you jump as high as a flea?

A tiny flea can jump as high as 12 inches!

Have a friend hold a ruler so that the end marked "0" is on the floor. Stand next to the ruler and jump as high as you can.

MORE FUN. Have your child find those family members who can jump higher than a flea and those who cannot.

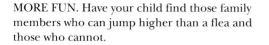

61

MATH FOCUS: ADDITION AND MULTIPLICATION. By using a calculator to explore "skip counting," children get hands-on practice of a pre-multiplication strategy that will help them understand the times tables.

Have available a calculator. Ask your child to press the appropriate keys as you read each problem aloud. Help your child solve the last problem by reminding him or her that each person has the same number of fingers.

What should she press on the calculator?
What numbers will she see?
How many fingers do 4 people have in all?

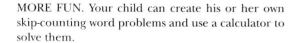

MORE FUN. Your child can create his or her own skip-counting word problems and use a calculator to solve them.

ANSWERS. She should press + 10. Then she should press = four times. She will see 10, 20, 30, 40. Four people have 40 fingers in all.

TIME-LIFE for CHILDREN ®

Publisher: Robert H. Smith
Associate Publisher and Managing Editor: Neil Kagan
Assistant Managing Editor: Patricia Daniels
Editorial Directors: Jean Burke Crawford, Allan Fallow,
    Karin Kinney, Sara Mark, Elizabeth Ward
Director of Marketing: Margaret Mooney
Product Managers: Cassandra Ford, Shelley L. Schimkus
Director of Finance: Lisa Peterson
Financial Analyst: Patricia Vanderslice
Administrative Assistant: Barbara A. Jones
Production Manager: Prudence G. Harris
Production: Celia Beattie
Supervisor of Quality Control: James King

Produced by Kirchoff/Wohlberg, Inc.

Series Director: Mary Jane Martin
Creative Director: Morris A. Kirchoff
Mathematics Director: Jo Dennis
Designer: Jessica A. Kirchoff
Assistant Designers: Brian Collins, Mariah Corrigan,
    Ann Eitzen, Judith Schwartz
Contributing Writers: Anne M. Miranda, Shereen Rutman
Managing Editor: Nancy Pernick
Editors: Susan M. Darwin, Beth Grout, David McCoy

Cover Illustration: Tom Leonard

CONSULTANTS

Mary Jane Martin spent 17 years working in elementary school classrooms as a teacher and reading consultant; for seven of those years she was a first-grade teacher. The second half of her career has been devoted to publishing. During this time she has helped create and produce a wide variety of innovative elementary programs, including two mathematics textbook series.

Jo Dennis has worked as a teacher and math consultant in England, Australia, and the United States for more than 20 years. Most recently, she has helped develop and write several mathematics textbooks for kindergarten, first grade, and second grade.

Catherine Motz Peterson is a curriculum specialist who spent five years developing an early elementary mathematics program for the nationally acclaimed Fairfax County Public Schools in Virginia. She is also mathematics consultant to the University Of Maryland, Catholic University, and the Fredrick County Public Schools in Maryland. Ms. Peterson is the director of the Capitol Hill Day School in Washington, D.C.

Theodore H. Weisse is an entomological consultant. He has taught in Long Island, New York, schools for more than 20 years. He is a trustee and a life member of the New York Entomological Society and a life member of the American Entomological Society.

Thomas D. Mullin directs the Hidden Oaks Nature Center in Fairfax County, Virginia, where he coordinates workshops and seminars designed to promote appreciation for wildlife and the environment. He is also the Washington representative for the National Association for Interpretation, a professional organization for naturalists involved in public education.

Library of Congress Cataloging-in-Publication Data
Right in your own backyard: nature math.
        p.   cm. —— (I love math)
        Summary: Stories, poems, activities, and games introduce readers to the rich array of math to be found in our own backyards.
        ISBN 0-8094-9962-2
        1. Mathematics—Juvenile literature. [1. Mathematics.
2. Nature study. 3. Mathematical recreations.] I. Time-Life for Children (Firm) II. Series.
QA40.5.R54   1992
510—dc20   92-27222
                                                                    CIP
                                                                    AC

A STONE'S THROW

The Number of Players: 2–4

The Object of the Game: To get rid of all of your counters or stones.

The Playing Pieces: One small stone for each player and 20 additional stones or counters (such as pennies or cereal pieces) for each player.

The Play: Each player gets one small stone and 20 counters. Place the game board on a table or any flat, steady surface. Players take turns throwing their small stones into the water. The number a player lands on tells that player how many counters he or she loses. For example, if a player lands on a three, that player loses three counters. A player gets to throw again if his or her stone lands on a line or goes off the board.

The Winner: The winner is the first player to lose all 20 counters. In this game, winning is losing.

Math Concepts: Understanding diminishing numbers. Subtracting from 20.